Mountain Rack Railways of Switzerland

by
J.R. Bardsley

THE OAKWOOD PRESS

British Library Cataloguing in Publication Data
A Record for this book is available from the British Library
ISBN 0 85361 511 X

Typeset by Oakwood Graphics.
Repro by Ford Graphics, Ringwood, Hants.
Printed by The Witney Press, Witney, Oxon.

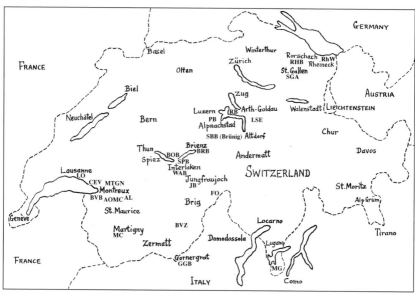

Front cover, top: The station at Schynige Platte, July 1975. — *Author*

Front cover, bottom: Brienz-Rothorn-Bahn trains in July 1975. — *Author*

Rear cover, top: A train from Andermatt arriving at Göschenen, July 1973. — *Author*

Rear cover, bottom: Jungfrau Bahn trains at Kleine Scheidegg, July 1975. — *Author*

Title page: The eastbound 'Glacier Express' on its way to Chur, July 1973. — *Author*

Published by
The Oakwood Press (Usk)
P.O. Box 13, Usk, Mon., NP15 1YS.

E-mail: oakwood-press@dial.pipex.com
Website: http://ds.dial.pipex.com/oakwood-press

Contents

The Rack-and-Pinion Railways

The Rack-and-Adhesion Railways

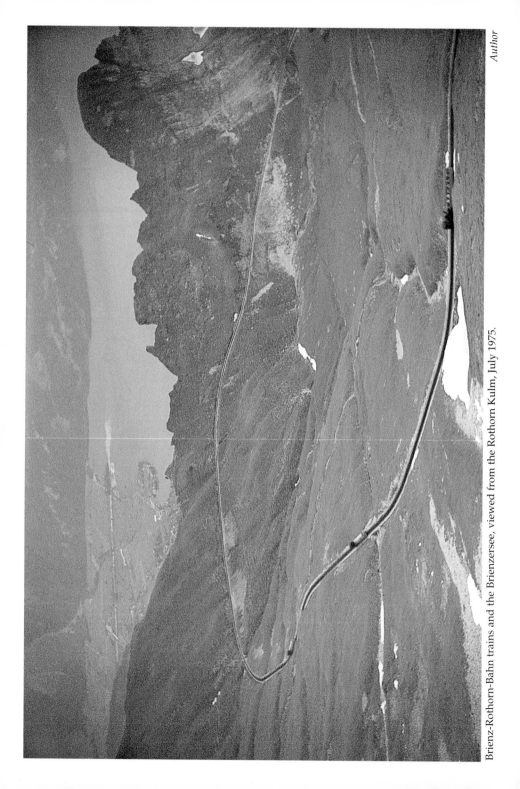

Brienz-Rothorn-Bahn trains and the Brienzersee, viewed from the Rothorn Kulm, July 1975.

Brienz-Rothorn-Bahn (BRB)

The small town of Brienz lies at the eastern end of the lake to which it gives its name, and ships of the Bern-Lötschberg-Simplon Railway make the journey from the landing-stage at Interlaken Ost to Brienz in 75 minutes. Only one paddle-steamer - the *Lötschberg*, which entered service in July, 1914 - now remains in service on the lake, and a voyage on this ship makes a perfect complement to a journey on the Brienz-Rothorn-Bahn (BRB). As the *Lötschberg* nears the landing-stage at Brienz, the traveller will see clouds of smoke billowing slowly into the sky behind the Brünig line station. There is no mistaking this evidence that locomotives of the BRB - three or four of them at busy times - are making ready for their next journey to the Rothorn on what was the last wholly steam-operated rack railway left in Switzerland until diesel locomotives were added to the stock in 1973.

Brünig line fast trains reach Brienz in 18 minutes from Interlaken Ost and in 101 minutes from Luzern, but the pleasantest way to approach the town is undoubtedly by ship.

The 800 mm gauge Brienz-Rothorn-Bahn, employing the rack and pinion system designed by Roman Abt in 1882, was opened in 1892. World War I dealt the railway a serious blow, the decline in traffic led to closure in 1915 and it did not re-open until 1931. The line is 4¾ miles in length and has a ruling gradient of 1 in 4. From Brienz, the initial climb is through woods and pastures, then comes a tunnel from which, through successive openings in the rock, there is a wonderful view of the lake. The engines take water at Planalp and are much photographed whilst doing so. At the height of summer, there is a procession of three or four trains for each booked journey in the timetable. To watch them from the summit station as the engines pound up the last mile of the line into the short tunnel near the top is a sight not to be missed.

The 10 steam engines of the BRB perform prodigious work throughout the summer. No. 1 ran on the Chemin de fer Glion-Naye until 1941 when it went to the Ferrovia Monte Generoso from whom it was bought in 1962. No. 5 came from the Wengernalpbahn where it worked until 1911. Three locomotives of revolutionary design numbered 12, 14 and 15 were bought from SLM-Winterthur, the first in 1992 and the others in 1996. They are oil-fired, and designed for single manning. On each upward journey of 55 minutes, they push their red coaches from the smoke-wreathed station at Brienz to the clear, wind-swept heights of the Rothorn Kulm, 7,378 feet above sea level, and, in so doing, surmount a greater difference in altitude between termini than any other Swiss mountain railway.

The Snowdon Mountain Railway, opened in 1896, is almost exactly the same length as the BRB, and employs seven of a similar type of locomotive. All were built by the Schweizerische Lokomotiv und Maschinen Fabrik, of Winterthur. If an engine and coach from the Swiss railway could be placed alongside an engine and coach from the Welsh, the two trains would be almost indistinguishable one from the other. The Brienzer Rothorn line, however, is steeper than the Snowdon, making an ascent of 5,515 feet compared with the Welsh line's 3,140 feet from Llanberis to Summit. Both railways afford their passengers a memorable experience, and a glimpse of mountain railway operation as it was before the turn of the century.

A stone at the summit of the Rothorn marks the meeting of the cantons of Bern, Luzern and Unterwalden.

A steam revival was launched when Swiss Locomotive and Machine Works at Winterthur brought out their revoltionary design for one man-operated locomotives for use on rack and pinion railways. The first bought by the BRB in 1992 is seen at the intermediate station of Planalp on 21st June, 1995. Two more were bought by the BRB in 1996 and four others are at work in Austria. *Alan Pike*

On an early autumn day in 1988, a train with 'panoramic' coaches waits for passengers from the Brunig line station nearby. The train will be pushed to a station close to the summit of the Rothorn by one of the three Hm 2t2 diesel locomotives, two of which entered service in 1975 and the third in 1987. *Alan Pike*

Schynige Platte Bahn (SPB)

A metre gauge Bernese Oberland Bahn train from Interlaken Ost makes the journey to Wilderswil in five minutes. Here the trains of the Schynige Platte Bahn, painted either red and cream, brown or green and propelled by small, 0-4-0 electric locomotives, wait in an adjoining platform to take travellers to the summit station. A surviving 0-4-2 steam engine - number 5 of 1894 - is used for some of the journeys in high summer, it is also used to remove some of the catenary at the end of the summer season and its reinstatement in the spring.

The line was opened in 1893 and absorbed by the Bernese Oberland Bahn in 1895. It is of 800 mm (2 ft 7½ in.) gauge and uses the Riggenbach/Pauli rack. The journey of 4½ miles is completed in 52 minutes, the ruling gradient being 1 in 4.

Breitlauenen, the passing station, is reached in half an hour and soon, as the train emerges from the Grätli tunnel, the magnificent chain of the central Bernese Oberland mountains comes into view. The Schynige Platte station lies at a height of 6,453 feet, and from it the prospect of the snowy peaks of the Eiger, Mönch and Jungfrau across the valley of the Schwarze Lütschine is unforgettably beautiful.

An easy footpath leads to the summit and, during the summer, an excellent alpine garden is reached from the end of the station platform.

Locomotive No. 5 of the Schynige Platte Bahn at Wilderswil in August 1937.

R.W. Kidner

A Schynige Platte Bahn train about to enter Grätli tunnel on its descent to Wilderswil, June 1973.

Author

A train from Wilderswil at the Schynige Platte terminus, June 1973.   *Author*

Left: Schynige Platte Bahn steam locomotive H2/3 No. 5 at Wilderswil, June 1973.   *Author*

Below: One of the beautifully restored sets of coaches of the Schynige Platte Bahn with its red and cream He2/2 locomotive at Wilderswil awaiting passengers for its journey to the summit station in September 1998.
Les Heath

A Wengernalpbahn train is seen leaving Alpiglen in August 1937.   *R.W. Kidner*

A busy scene at Alpiglen, between Grindelwald and Kleine Scheidegg, with four down trains crammed into the loop in August 1937.   *R.W. Kidner*

Wengernalpbahn (WAB)

The Wengernalpbahn, which links the towns of Grindelwald and Lauterbrunnen, via a summit point at Kleine Scheidegg, is one of the most remarkable lines in Europe. For the whole of its route, the giant peaks of the Bernese Oberland keep it company - the Eiger towering above it at its eastern end, Mönch at its centre skyline and the Jungfrau its incomparable companion to the west.

The railway, built with a gauge of 800 mm (2 ft 7½ in.) and the Riggenbach/Pauli rack system, was opened in 1893. Some 12 miles in length, it forms the centre section of a complex of lines which connect Interlaken with the Jungfraujoch. The northernmost section, the metre-gauge Berner Oberland Bahn, takes the traveller from Interlaken Ost to Zweilütschinen; here it divides, one branch proceeding up the valley of the Schwarze Lütschine to Grindelwald, the other up the Weise Lütschine gorge to Lauterbrunnen. Then comes the Wengernalpbahn; and the final stage, from Kleine Scheidegg to the Jungfraujoch, is provided by the Jungfrau Bahn.

Of the two climbs to Kleine Scheidegg, that from Grindelwald is the steeper and shorter. From Lauterbrunnen, the original line to Wengen is now used only for freight traffic for part of its length, for in 1910 a new stretch with an easier ruling gradient - 1 in 5½ - was built. Wengen is a delightful resort, situated more than 4,000 feet above sea level and relying entirely on the railway for all communication with the outside world. Kleine Scheidegg, at 6,762 feet, is the focal point of the line, busy summer and winter alike. Here the older green and cream coaches of the Wengernalpbahn and the 1988-built green and bright yellow units, share the station with the orange and cream and sometimes the old brown vehicles of the Jungfrau Bahn.

On fine days in summer, two or three trains, perhaps even four, will be necessary for each scheduled departure from both Grindelwald and Lauterbrunnen, the journey from the former to Kleine Scheidegg taking 35 minutes, and that from the latter 45 minutes. Up to seven trains are necessary for each departure at peak times in winter. In the years of steam before World War I, these timings were just twice their present length; and how one wishes that they, and the locomotives which propelled them, could have been with us yet.

Wengernalpbahn trains at Kleine Scheidegg, July 1975.   *Author*

A scene at Lauterbrunnen station in July 1975.　　　　　　*Author*

A Wengernalpbahn train from Lauterbrunnen climbing to Kleine Scheidegg, July 1975. *Author*

Berner Oberland Bahn and Wengernalpbahn trains at Grindelwald station in July 1975.

Author

A Wengernalp Bahn train in Wengen station, July 1975.   *Author*

Kleine Scheidegg, with Wengernalpbahn and Jungfrau Bahn trains in July 1975. *Author*

Two of the four 2-car units delivered in 1988, led by BDeh 4/8 131, arrive at Wengen from Kleine Scheidegg on 25th July, 1990. *Alan Pike*

Two views of Jungfrau Bahn trains at Kleine Scheidegg in July 1975. *Author*

Jungfrau Bahn (JB)

For ever above the snow-line, the station at Jungfraujoch is the highest in Europe, 11,333 feet above sea level. Half a million people come here annually in the electric motor-coaches which climb the 4,500 feet from Kleine Scheidegg. The metre-gauge line, fitted with the Strub rack, is 5¾ miles long, and the orange and cream and brown cars make the ascent in 51 minutes, including five-minute stops at the tunnel stations of Eigerwand and Eismeer. An extra minute is allowed in summer.

The Jungfrau Bahn was the vision which became reality of a Zürich engineer, Dr Adolph Guyer-Zeller. It was begun in 1896 and opened throughout 16 years later, on 1st August, 1912. Like the Gornergratbahn the railway uses a 3 phase supply, since 1964 1,125v 50Hz. The total cost was £714,000 - twelve million francs in the days before 1914. Sad to say, Dr Guyer-Zeller did not live to see the full realisation of his dream, for he died in 1899.

From the station shared with the Wengernalp Bahn at Kleine Scheidegg, the Jungfrau Bahn (JB) trains run at first in the open air, but beyond Eigergletscher they enter the 4½ mile tunnel in which they remain for the rest of the journey. This great tunnel through the rock of the Eiger and Mönch is 14 feet high and 12 feet wide. The first underground station, Eigerwand, has a gallery with windows cut into the north face of the Eiger which give a wonderful view of Grindelwald, nearly 6,000 feet below, and of Lake Thun and the distant mountains beyond.

The line then curves through more than 90 degrees to reach Eismeer, the second station in the tunnel, and here the view from the rock-face windows is south-eastward, to the towering peaks of the Wetterhorn, Schreckhorn and Fiescherhorn, the Aletsch glacier and snowfields. One of the 'windows' features in the book *Eiger Sanction*, later made into a film featuring Clint Eastwood.

From the upper terminus of the railway at Jungfraujoch, a lift takes the traveller to an observation terrace on the Sphinx, which is situated on the saddle between Mönch and the Jungfrau. From here the views are of unimaginable beauty and splendour northward to Interlaken and its lakes, and the hills of central Switzerland; south-eastward to the Jungfraufirn and Aletsch glacier, a river of ice and snow that sweeps down in a wide, magnificent curve to Belalp, which is no more than five miles from Brig; and to north-east and south-west the gleaming, snow-covered peaks of Mönch and the Jungfrau.

Who could ask more than the combination of an enthralling railway journey and a destination with views to every point of the compass surely unsurpassed in the world?

Memorial to Dr Adolph Guyer-Zeller.   *Author*

17

The combined station of the Wengernalp Bahn and the JB is seen from a train as it climbs toward the Eigergletscher station before entering the long tunnel to the summit. Since the picture was taken on 17th August, 1988, several new apartments have been built near the station. *Alan Pike*

A train nears the end of its descent from the Jungfraujoch on 17th August, 1988 as it approaches Kleine Scheidegg. The high fencing is to prevent skiers from hurtling onto the tracks! *Alan Pike*

A He2/2, one of a batch of four delivered by SLM of Winterthur in 1912, waits at the Jungfraujoch station with its superbly maintained matching coach in August 1988.   *Alan Pike*

One of the older units of the Jungfraubahn, named 'Euro Tunnel' seen in September 1998.
Les Heath

At Kleine Scheidegg on 18th April, 1999, skiers load their skis on the rack specially fitted on a flat wagon bearing the legend 'Ski- Express Eigergletscher'. The station bearing the glacier's name is the final one before trains enter the long tunnel which climbs to the Jungfraujoch.

Alan Pike

One of the new Jungfraubahn units at Kleine Scheidegg waiting to leave for the Jungfraujoch station, the highest in Europe, on 7th September, 1998.   *Les Heath*

Lausanne-Ouchy Railway (LO)

The Chemin de fer Lausanne-Ouchy links the centre of Lausanne with its port on Lac Léman (Lake Geneva). It is a mile in length and has three intermediate stations, the journey between termini taking six minutes.

An uninterrupted shuttle service between the two uppermost stations - the terminus at Lausanne-Flon and the Swiss Federal Railways' (CFF) station - is run between the hours of 06.30 and 21.00. The service to Ouchy continues until 23.20.

The line, opened in 1877, was originally a cable-worked funicular, and was the first such railway in Switzerland. Lausanne Gare to Flon was converted to rack and pinion (Strub) in 1954; Lausanne Flon to Ouchy was converted in 1958. It shares a station at Flon with the standard gauge Tramway de Sud-Ouest Lausannois (TSOL), a standard gauge line which opened in 1991. It will be joined (in 1999) by the metre gauge C de F Lausanne-Echalllens-Bercher. The blue and cream trains run for part of their journey in a spacious, airy tunnel and, for the remainder, along a route bordered for much of its way by trees. Ouchy is the busiest port on the lake, and a place of great charm, with lovely gardens and promenades, and a profusion of tropical plants. Byron and Shelley stayed at the Ancre, predecessor of the Hotel d'Angleterre, in 1816, and here Byron wrote 'The Prisoner of Chillon'.

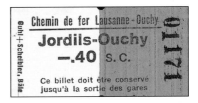

This November 1998 view shows units which operate a shuttle service partly underground between Lausanne Ouchy and Lausanne SBB station. *Les Heath*

The single car, one of two built in 1964, stands at Lausanne Gare on the shuttle service to Lausanne Flon, a distance of only 294 metres (321 yards), in November 1998. *Alan Pike*

This unit is seen at Ouchy station on 18th September, 1998, which is the works depot for repair etc. *Les Heath*

Chemin de fer Montreux-Territet-Glion-Naye (MTGN)

The station at Montreux is shared by trains of the Swiss Federal Railways, the metre-gauge Montreux-Oberland Bernois (MOB) line and the 800 mm rack railway which ascends to the Rochers-de-Naye, where the terminus is 6,460 feet above sea level. The blue and cream coaches take 55 minutes to make the journey of 6½ miles, travelling by way of Glion and Caux. Glion is the upper station of a funicular which makes the ascent of 978 feet from Territet, now a suburb of Montreux, in a time of four minutes. The gradient is steeper than 1 in 2. This funicular is interesting in that it is one of only a few which make use of water-ballast tanks as their means of propulsion - a fact which accounts for the audible ebb and flow of water before the commencement of each journey. Glion and Caux have become favourite residential areas for citizens of Montreux, and the Rochers-de-Naye timetable confirms this, for many of the trains run between Montreux and Caux only.

The line was opened from Glion to Rochers-de-Naye on 16th September, 1892 and was steam worked until 12th July, 1938. Steam returned to the line in 1992 following the delivery of a new locomotive from SLM-Winterthur which operates services spring and autumn between Caux and Rochers-de-Naye. With a ruling gradient of 1 in 4½, and equipped with the Abt rack, the railway climbs to a summit station set in a bowl, possibly an extinct volcanic crater, near the summit. In spring and summer, it is ablaze with wildflowers and in winter, the snow attracts many skiers. It is also popular with para-sailers. A tunnel through the mountain connects the station with a restaurant giving superb views over Lac Léman. The highest point of the Rochers is some minutes' walk from the station, and from it there is also a wonderful prospect of Lac Léman and the mountain peaks to the east and south. In very bad weather, trains between Caux and the terminus at Rochers-de-Naye may be cancelled.

The section between Montreux and Glion opened on 8th April, 1909 and was electrically operated from the outset. The amalgamated lines have long been part of the MOB.

A very early photograph of the summit station at Rochers-de-Naye, possibly taken prior to opening. The tall building to the right is the Grand Hotel.   *R.W. Kidner Collection*

Another very early view of the Rochers-de-Naye line with two of the steam locomotives that operated to the summit until 1938. The men standing by the trackbed suggest that this view may predate the official opening of this section of the line.   *R.W. Kidner Collection*

The Abt system 0-4-2T *Lausanne* of the Rochers-de-Naye line at Glion in June 1938.

R.W. Kidner

A mixed electric train on the newly electrified track at Glion in June 1938.   *R.W. Kidner*

A test electric train from Rochers-de-Naye arrives at Caux on 11th June, 1938 when this section of the line was still steam-worked.
R.W. Kidner

HGe 2/2 dates from the opening of the line in 1909 and is seen at Montreux on 23rd May, 1976. It was still used occasionally on passenger work but mostly on permanent way work. It was still in service in 1997.
Alan Pike

Rolling stock of the Rochers-de-Naye line at Glion station in July 1973. *Author*

Two units of the type introduced in 1983 display at the left the old livery and at the right the darker new livery. There is no need to shelter the trains under cover on 15th August, 1993 as it is in winter when deep snow covers these popular ski slopes. *Alan Pike*

From spring to autumn this modern, oil fired, steam rack tank locomotive built by SLM in 1992 pushes two vintage carriages from Caux up to Rochers-de-Naye where it is seen on 15th August, 1993.   *Alan Pike*

One of the newer units at Rochers-de-Naye on 20th September, 1998. Splendid views over Lake Geneva can be had from here.   *Les Heath*

Gornergratbahn (GGB)

Brig, situated on the Rhône at the northern end of the Simplon tunnels, is an ideal town for the railway enthusiast. Into its main station come trains of the Swiss Federal Railways' Simplon line and of the Bern-Lötschberg-Simplon Railway; and in the square outside the station the red metre-gauge trains of the Furka-Oberalp (FO) and the Brig-Visp-Zermatt Bahn (BVZ) arrive and depart. A BVZ express will make the journey up the valley of the Matter Visp river to Zermatt in 80 minutes. From Zermatt the first electric mountain rack railway in the world ascends to the highest open-air station in Europe - Gornergrat. Opened in 1898, and lengthened to a new upper terminus in 1909, this metre-gauge line is 5¾ miles in length and has a ruling gradient of 1 in 5. It employs 725v 50Hz 3 phase current requiring two separate contact wires and recently, new high capacity two-car sets have been introduced to cope with the increasing numbers of skiers in winter. It twists and turns so frequently that its profile on the map resembles that of a length of string dropped carelessly on the ground.

Using the Abt rack system, the bronze-coloured Gornergrat Bahn trains take 43 minutes to climb to the Gornergrat, 10,134 feet above sea level, with four stops on the way. Not far from Zermatt, the Findelen Gorge is crossed by a fine cantilever viaduct, with a gradient of 1 in 8; and there are four short tunnels on the lower stages of the line. The Matterhorn in all its unique beauty is in full view for much of the journey.

From the summit, which overlooks the lovely valley of the Gorner glacier, the glittering panorama to the south - of Monte Rosa (which is topped by the highest point on Swiss soil, the Dufour Peak, 15,203 ft), Lyskamm, Castor, Pollux and Breithorn - is truly wonderful. Beyond the natural frontier of their peaks lies Italy.

GGB No. 7, a rack tank used in the construction of the line, was photographed on 2nd May, 1998 plinthed outside Zermatt station during the centenary celebrations of the opening of the railway. After passing to the Glion-Naye railway, it finished up on a Spanish railway whence it was loaned for the occasion. *Alan Pike*

A Gornergrat Bahn train *en route* from Zermatt to Gornergrat in 1973.   *Author*

Gornergrat - the highest open-air station in Europe backed by Monte Rosa in June 1973.   *Author*

A train from Gornergrat swings past the depot at Zermatt on the last stage of its journey on 16th August, 1993. *Alan Pike*

Bhe 4/8 3051 is one of a batch of four units delivered by SLM in 1993. These are permitted to ascend or descend at 28 kmh almost twice the previous top speed. On 2nd May, 1998 it is in the early stage of its journey to Gornergrat as it passes Findelbach. *Alan Pike*

Two views of the Ferrovia Monte Generoso trains at Generoso Vetta in July 1975.

(Both) Author

Ferrovia Monte Generoso (MG)

Lugano station, on the Gotthard line, is situated high above the town that is set so beautifully by the lake; and from the station a funicular descends to a small, sheltered square - the Piazza Funicolare - not far from the lakeside road. The ships of the Società Navigazione del Lago di Lugano ply on several routes, and one of these is to Capolago Lago, the lower terminus of the 800 mm gauge Ferrovia del Monte Generoso.

The ships for Capolago leave from Lugano Centrale and it is best to take the 09.15 departure. The leisurely journey takes about an hour and for part of the time the upper terminus of the Monte Generoso railway at Generosa Vetta is visible, perched near the mountain summit to the east of the lake. The lower terminus adjoins the Capolago landing-stage. The journey from Lugano can also be made via the Gotthard line and takes 16 minutes, the train sweeping down through Paradiso to the lake, then across the Melide causeway, in company with the motorway, to Capolago-Riva San Vitale. Here, a short distance from the lakeside terminus, the Monte Generoso train is joined.

Originally steam-operated by engines using the Abt rack and pinion system, diesel railcars were introduced in 1953, the only ones of their kind in Switzerland. The line was opened in 1889. It is 5½ miles long and rises from an altitude of 896 feet at the lakeside to one of 5,223 feet at the summit station. The maximum gradient is 1 in 4½. In 1982, the line was electrified at 650v DC and uses two-car sets seating 96 people. During the years when steam locomotives provided the power, the journey took 75 minutes; most trains now take 37 up and 40 down. Financial problems led to the closure of the line in 1939 but the owner of a large store chain in Switzerland bought it and two years later it was re-opened.

From Capolago, the line winds southward for some distance before turning to the north towards Bella Vista. The motor-coach's searchlight illuminates the tunnels as they come and go, as though the sun were shining brightly into them. At first, the views are restricted by the woods through which the line passes, but during the last quarter of an hour of the journey, from Bella Vista onwards, they become more open. The buildings at the terminus, recently much improved and enlarged, stand on the edge of a precipice, 250 feet below the summit of Monte Generoso. At the mountain top, a white post marks the border between Switzerland and Italy, and one wishes that all frontiers could be as peaceful and as easily crossed as this one. The view westward to the peaks of Monte Rosa is unforgettable, and on a clear day Milan cathedral is visible, more than 30 miles distant across the plain of Lombardy.

A steam locomotive of the Ferrovia Monte Generoso has been preserved, and stood for many years outside the station at Capolago, it has been restored and (in 1999) works on Saturdays in July and August on special trains.

The service is sparse, and a careful check should be made as to the departure point, and whether the advertised service will operate, because in poor weather, or sometimes due to inadequate patronage, services can be cancelled.

A preserved steam locomotive of the Ferrovia Monte Generoso at Capolago in July 1975.

Author

Bhe 4/8 13 stands in the 'station' at Capolago Riva San Vitale, not far from the Federal Railways' station on 22nd October, 1989. The line is the only rack railway to be operated by steam, diesel and, from 1992, electric traction.

Alan Pike

Pilatus-Bahn (PB)

Pilatus, for so long the inspiration of legend, dominates the skyline to the south of Luzern, and up its southern slopes climbs the steepest rack railway in the world. No more than 2⅔ miles in length, it starts at an altitude of 1,434 feet at Alpnachstad and ascends 5,344 feet to the summit station. Such a line demands gradients of no mean order, and the most formidable is indeed almost 1 in 2.

The railway was opened in 1889. The rack in use is unique to the Pilatus system and was designed by the engineer of the line, Edouard Locher-Freuler, to cope with the exceptional gradients. Steam rail-cars were used until 15th May, 1937, when electrification came. The journey-time was then reduced from 70 to 30 minutes, partly by the elimination of the stop to enable the engine to take water at Amsigenalp, the passing station. Two steam railcars have survived to the present day, one of which can be seen in the fine transport museum in Luzern.

The ship from Luzern to Alpnachstad makes several calls *en route*, zig-zagging across the western end of the lake to do so. As the steamer approaches the low bridge beyond which lies the Alpnachersee, the masts are lowered and the funnel slowly telescopes. The vessel glides on through the strait, a few stopping at Rotzloch, then turns towards Alpnachstad on the final stage of the voyage.

Brünig line trains make the journey from Luzern in 20 minutes, and that from Interlaken Ost in two hours. At Alpnachstad, the Pilatus train waits in its own station across the road. The platform of this station is so steep that it is built in the form of steps, and the electric motor-coaches, painted red, are built to a similar alignment so that the seats remain level during the journey. As points would be unsafe for use with such steep lines, traversers are used at Alpnachstad, Amsigenalp and Pilatus Kulm, the upper terminus. These consist of complete sections of track which are moved from side to side electrically, that at Alpnachstad transferring the coaches from line to line in readiness for the next journey, the two at Amsigenalp controlling the 'passing loop' and that at Pilatus Kulm selecting the platform road.

The steepness of the lines when first seen at Alpnachstad makes one wonder how steam-powered vehicles ever managed to climb such a gradient. Yet for nearly 50 years they did so, clawing their way up from the terminus, as the electric cars do now so smoothly, through peaceful, tree-shaded meadows to the bare upper reaches of the mountain. The final stage of the journey, round the precipitous face of the Esel, provides a truly memorable experience.

The summit of the Esel is 300 feet above the station. The highest peak of Pilatus, the Tomlishorn, which can be reached by a footpath, commands a splendid view of the Bernese Oberland peaks and no less than 14 lakes.

Pilatus-Bahn coaches on the last stage of their ascent to Pilatus Kulm in July 1973.   *Author*

This is *not* the steepest section of the track as a 'train' approaches the two-track terminus at Pilatus Kulm on 11th August, 1997.   *Alan Pike*

Top left: A Pilatus-Bahn coach at the Amsigenalp passing loop in July 1973. *Author*

Top right: A train approaches one of the traversers on the line which are used in the place of conventional pointwork, 11th August, 1997. *Alan Pike*

Above: The tilt on the cabs of this snow plough and works vehicle built in 1981 looks curious as the vehicle stands on the traverser at the depot at Alpnachstad on 21st April, 1991. The only level track on the railway is at this depot. *Alan Pike*

Locomotive No. 7 restored by SLM to celebrate the 125th anniversary of the Vitznau-Rigi Bahn is seen in August 1997. The train is just approaching the summit station at Rigi Kulm. The line in the foreground is the Arth-Rigi route from Arth Goldau. From Rigi Staffel both lines run side by side to the summit at Rigi Kulm. *Les Heath*

The 'power car' of a unit dating from the electrification in 1907 stands in front of the entrance to the 'Hotel Montana' in Luzern on 19th August, 1997. From this entrance, a funicular takes guests to the reception area and other levels of the hotel. *Alan Pike*

Rigi Bahnen (RB)

A Gotthard line train from Luzern takes the traveller to Arth- Goldau in 25 minutes. Here, on a bridge over the main lines, is the lower terminus of the Arth-Rigi Bahn (ARB), opened in 1875. The blue and cream coaches take 37 minutes to reach the summit station of Rigi Kulm, an ascent of more than 4,000 feet. The line is built to the standard gauge and is 5⅓ miles in length, with a maximum gradient of 1 in 5.

Rigi Staffel and the summit station are shared with the Vitznau-Rigi Bahn (VRB). The two railways merged in 1992 to form Rigi Bahnen. The VRB opened to Rigi-Staffel - where it meets the erstwhile ARB - in 1871 and to the summit in 1873. It was the first mountain rack railway to be built in Europe, and only the second in the world. It is a standard gauge line, like its counterpart the ARB, and its red coaches make the journey of 4¼ miles from Vitznau, on the Vierwaldstättersee (Lake Lucerne), to the summit in 30 minutes. The two lines enable one to make a circular journey from Luzern to the Rigi and back, the last lap being by ship from Vitznau. Two in eight summer services are operated by a paddle-steamer, for, happily, the Swiss Paddle-Steamer Preservation Society has acquired a majority holding in the Lake Lucerne Ship Company (SGV). To board a ship like the *Gallia* after descending from the Rigi Kulm, and to watch its machinery at work and see the perfection of its great cranks and connecting-rods as they drive the vessel forward, is the happiest way to end a visit to the Rigi. The *Gallia* which entered service in July 1913, was completely renovated in 1977, and is the fastest paddle-steamer on any European lake.

The two Rigi lines use the rack system designed by Niklaus Riggenbach, the Swiss engineer who was the driving force behind the Vitznau line. The first locomotives numbered 1-6 were built at Olten and had vertical boilers. No. 7 of a similar type was built by SLM and was their first locomotive and was supplied in 1873. It was in the Luzern Transport Museum and was restored to working order for the second time, spending the summers of 1996 and 1997 on the line. Electrification came to the ARB in 1906 and to the VRB 31 years later, but steam locomotives still take their coaches from Vitznau up to Rigi Kaltbad on Wednesdays and Saturdays in summer. The two engines used for these turns are numbers 16 and 17, built by SLM in 1923 and 1925 respectively.

In the more leisurely days of the 19th century, people taking the Grand Tour would stay in one of the many hotels situated on the Rigi, for the sight of the sunrise from the mountain was one of the highlights of the tour. The first hotel was opened in 1816, and in the heyday of the Rigi's popularity, which lasted for the best part of a hundred years, guests were welcomed in more than a dozen hotels. In those days, Luzern was a quiet lakeside resort, and it was the mountain that was as busy as an anthill. There was even an adhesion railway, worked by steam locomotives, to enable travellers to reach hotels at Rigi-Scheidegg; it left the Vitznau line at Rigi-Kaltbad and the trains took between 30 and 35 minutes to make the journey. The hotels have gone now, and the railway with them. However, much of the track is now a footpath and a coach remains as a private dwelling.

An Arth Rigi Bahn train at Arth-Goldau in July 1973.   *Author*

Ex-Arth Rigi BDhe 2/4 of 1949 stands at Rigi Kulm on 20th August, 1996. The two railways retained their respective colour schemes after the merger in 1992, the Vitznau-Rigi being red and white.   *Alan Pike*

A Vitznau-Rigi Bahn train at the Rigi Kulm in July 1973. *Author*

Restored VRB locomotive No. 7 is seen alongside one of the modern units in its striking red and pink livery at Rigi Staffel in August 1997. On the left is the ARB line. It is from this point that the two lines run parrallel to the terminus at Rigi Kulm. *Les Heath*

Bhe 4/4 22 together with a driving trailer of the erstwhile Vitznau-Rigi Bahn arrives at Rigi Staffel on 20th August, 1996. *Alan Pike*

The ship station for the Lake Luzern boats forms the background for Bhe 4/4 21 on 14th August, 1997 as it runs onto the turntable giving access to the depot at Vitznau. *Alan Pike*

Rheineck-Walzenhausen Bahn (RhW)

The little town of Rheineck is situated on the Alter Rhein, close to the Bodensee and the Austrian border. From it, a rack railway leads up to the resort of Walzenhausen, and in doing so makes an ascent of 873 feet in 1⅕ miles. The ruling gradient is 1 in 4 and the upward journey is completed in six minutes, the downward in nine.

The line was built in 1896 as a cable-operated funicular, but, like the Lausanne-Ouchy, was converted in 1958 to rack and pinion (Riggenbach) working. A tramway was opened from the foot of the incline to Rheineck station in 1909. This was converted to rack in 1958 to enable through running. The service is operated by a single red 4-wheel electric motor-coach, which has its own small shed at Rheineck although the car is usually kept overnight at Walzenhausen station. The line is managed by the RHB.

The solitary item of rolling stock on the Rheineck-Walzenhausen Bahn was built by SLM in 1958 and is seen on 2nd March, 1999.   *Les Heath*

A Luzern to Interlaken Ost train at Brünig-Hasliberg in July 1973.   *Author*

A class '101' rolls down the rack section into Giswil with a modest load from Interlaken Ost on 21st May, 1952.   *Alan Pike*

Schweizerische Bundesbahnen (SBB)
Brünig Section

This metre-gauge line is the only part of the Swiss Federal Railway (SBB) which incorporates rack-and-pinion working for its steepest sections. The line runs between Luzern and Interlaken, and is 45¾ miles in length. It was worked by steam locomotives until 1942, when electrification brought a considerable reduction in the time allowed for the journey.

The first section between Alpnachstad and Brienz was built Jura-Bern-Luzern (JBL) and opened on 14th June, 1888 followed by Luzern to Alpnachstad on 1st June, 1889. It was taken over by the Jura-Simplon (JS) on 1st January, 1890. The line was completed between Brienz-Interlaken Ost by the SBB on 23rd August, 1916.

Trains leave Luzern and run southward by the lake to Hergiswil, where the Luzern-Stans-Engelberg line to Engelberg turns away. The next station is Alpnachstad, where the lower terminus of the Pilatus-Bahn is situated, as well as that for the steamers which arrive from Luzern. Five miles on, the train reaches Sarnen, the chief town of the canton of Obwalden. In the archives of the Rathaus is the *Weisses Buch*, a document of 1470 in which the history of the origins of the Swiss Confederation is to be found. The first section of Riggenbach rack-and-pinion track begins at Giswil and continues almost to Kaiserstuhl, then come two more before Brünig-Hasliberg is reached at a height of 3,287 feet, and the descent to Meiringen begins. This involves long stretches of rack-and-pinion working, but in spite of the difference in level of 1,335 feet between the summit and Meiringen, the journey is accomplished in 15 minutes.

At Meiringen, where reversal of trains is necessary, one of the Brünig line pinion-fitted steam locomotives, 0-6-0T No. 1068, built in 1926, is preserved outside the station. Another of the same class, No. 1067 built in 1910 is in working order as is No. 208 a 2-6-0T built in 1914 but not equipped for working on the rack, both of which were bought by the 'Friends of Steam Locos, Meiringen' in 1965. All were built by SLM. Nearby, the Reichenbach funicular ascends in five minutes from its lower station to the Upper Reichenbach Falls, where the fictional characters Sherlock Holmes and Professor Moriarty fought to resolve The Final Problem. Westward towards Interlaken, the town of Brienz is famous as a centre of wood carving, and has a school to teach this craft and another devoted to the art of violin-making.

Brienz is at the foot of the Brienz Rothorn Bahn. Outside the station, a bus can be taken to Ballenberg nearby, which has a growing collection of buildings transported from all parts of Switzerland and rebuilt in delightful surroundings.

In 1999, the best Brünig line trains take 1 hour 46 minutes to make the journey from Luzern to Interlaken Ost, including four minutes for the reversal at Meiringen. New locomotives came into use in 1986, with an hourly rating of 2,547 hp. Built by SLM, they are identical with those subsequently bought by the Furka-Oberalp, where they went in 1990 after delivery to the Brünig in 1989/90 of eight locomotives based on these prototypes.

A train for Luzern headed by HGe 101 965 *Lungern* is about to leave Giswil on 21st May, 1992. Sister locomotive No. 967, both of which entered service in 1990, stands alongside the engine shed. Beyond the station, trains enter the rack sections to climb to Brünig-Hasliberg. *Alan Pike*

Both HGe 101 966 and a Deh 4/6 in original livery are engaged in train assembly at Meiringen on 25th April, 1997. Trains reverse here either to tackle the climb to Brünig-Hasliberg or to go on their way to Interlaken Ost. *Alan Pike*

Chemins de fer Électriques Veveysans (CEV)

A general view of Blonay station on 15th August, 1993 looking toward Vevey. The commencement of the rack line to Les Pléiades is at the extreme right.   *Alan Pike*

The CEV is a metre gauge line formed by the amalgamation of two small companies in 1902. The section, adhesion operated, which connects Vevey, a resort on the northern shore of Lac Léman, with Blonay was opened on 1st October, 1902. The section from Blonay to Les Pléiades is equipped with Strub rack and pinion and opened on 8th July, 1911. Currently (1999) five power cars are pinion fitted. The line, three miles in length and with a ruling gradient of 1 in 5, ascends for nearly 2,400 feet to reach the upper terminus - 4,422 feet above sea level - and the trains take 20 minutes to make the journey.

From the summit at Les Pléiades, the views of the lake and of the Alpine peaks to the east and the Mont Blanc group to the south, are renowned.

The CEV became part of the Montreux Oberland Bernois Bahn on 1st January, 1990.

BDeh 2/4 73 built in 1970 awaits its next turn of duty at Blonay on 15th August, 1993.
Alan Pike

A train from Les Pléiades to Vevey approaches Blonay on 28th August, 1996.   *Alan Pike*

BE4/4 74 at Les Pléiades awaiting departure down to Blonay on 27th April, 1998   *Les Heath*

Luzern-Stans-Engelberg Bahn (LSE)

Originally, this metre-gauge railway, opened on 5th October, 1898, extended only from Stansstad to Engelberg, until the decision was taken to extend it over the narrow entrance to the Alpnachersee, so enabling a junction to be made at Hergiswil with the Brünig line. This extension, completed on 19th December, 1964 involved the construction of a rail tunnel 1,743 metres (1,906 yds) long, a shorter road tunnel and a reinforced concrete bridge, which also incorporates a dual carriageway for road traffic to take the place of the former swing-bridge. With the completion of the line to Hergiswil, the 850 volts three-phase current of the one-time Stansstad-Engelberg route was changed to the standard Swiss Federal supply at 15,000 volts16-7Hz.

The route involves normal adhesion working as far as Obermatt, but here the gradient steepens to 1 in 4 and the Riggenbach rack-and-pinion comes into operation until Gherst is reached. Soon the line emerges into a lovely valley, and comes to an end in the little town of Engelberg, 3,346 feet above sea level, and dominated by a number of magnificent peaks. The three-coach trains, painted red with white lettering, take an average of 55 minutes for the journey from Luzern, and slightly longer for the return.

The Benedictine Abbey of Engelberg was founded in 1120, and for centuries the monastery owned the whole village, until the French invasion in 1798. The abbey was burnt down on three occasions, and the present church and its adjoining quadrangular buildings were reconstructed between the years 1730 and 1737. The church organ is one of the largest in Switzerland, and is said to have ten thousand pipes.

A Luzern-Stans-Engelberg train in Luzern station in July 1973   *Author*

Diesel Gm4/4 111 named *Jumbo* stands near the weighbridge at Stansstad on 20th April, 1999.
Alan Pike

LSE Bdeh4/4 3 dating from 1964 stands at the terminus at Engelberg with a magnificent mountain backdrop on 20th April, 1999.   *Alan Pike*

Bernese Oberland Bahn (BOB)

The metre-gauge Bernese Oberland Railway opened on 1st July, 1890 with steam locomotives, and was electrified on 17th March, 1914 at 1,500v DC. It starts from Interlaken Ost station and proceeds via Wilderswil, where one can change for the Schynigge Platte Bahn, and the gorge of the Lütschine to Zweilütschinen, a distance of five miles. Here its trains divide. The portion for Lauterbrunnen, travelling up the valley of the Weise Lütschine, encounters two rack-and-pinion sections before reaching its destination, where huge cliffs and the majestic Jungfrau tower above the station.

The second portion of the train from Interlaken Ost proceeds up the Schwarze Lütschine valley to Grindelwald, again with the aid of two stretches of rack-and-pinion. At both Lauterbrunnen and Grindelwald, passengers wishing to travel further must leave their Bernese Oberland train for one of the Wengernalp Bahn because of the difference in gauge between the two. The latter provides one of the most spectacular routes in Europe in the 12 miles it covers between Lauterbrunnen and Grindelwald.

Since 1944, the Bernese Oberland, Wengernalp and Jungfrau Bahnen have operated under a joint agreement, with a head office in Interlaken. Their services are perfectly integrated, and must have given pleasure and wonderment to millions.

Shunting operations in progress at Zweilütschinen. *Author*

ABeh4/4″ 312 built in 1986 on the loop at Grindelwald on 7th March, 1989. The track of the Wengernalpbahn is just visible to the left in this view. *Alan Pike*

A train for Interlaken Ost is about to leave the terminal station at Grindelwald on 6th October, 1993. The small shed at the right belongs to the BOB. Note the small gap at the top of the doors to allow the contact wire to pass through. The Wengernalp Bahn is alongside the BOB to the right. *Alan Pike*

Chemin de fer Aigle-Ollon-Monthey-Champéry (AOMC)

The town of Aigle lies some 10 miles south of Montreux, on the Swiss Federal Railways main line between Lausanne and Brig, and thence to Domodossola in Italy via the Simplon tunnel. The red and white liveried trains of the line to Champéry start from the square outside the station at Aigle, then proceed in and alongside public roads to Ollon. Here the line turns in a south-westerly direction and crosses, in succession, the Simplon line, the river Rhône and the St Gingolph-St Maurice railway, passes the trailing junction for Champéry, and soon afterwards reaches Monthey-Ville.

After a stop which can vary considerably in length, the train restarts in reverse - for Monthey-Ville is a terminus. This can require a change of train, passengers having to transfer to waiting pinion-equipped railcars unless travelling in a 'through' coach. In recent years (to 1999) the tendency is to use adhesion-only railcars between Aigle and Monthey-Ville. Passengers for Champéry retrace their steps to Monthey-en-Place, passing the depot at the right before the train diverges to join the rack. This is the first of three rack-and-pinion sections which help it to climb high above the Val d'Illiez on a gradient of 1 in 7½. The village of the same name is a good place to pause. It is, even in 1999, hardly spoilt by modern development. Small restaurants offer good country fare at reasonable prices!

Now the Dents du Midi, whose highest peak is at 10,696 feet, are magnificently seen at the head of the valley, and before long, a second and a third length of rack-and-pinion bring the train to Champéry. The village lies at a height of 3,451 feet above sea level, and the journey of 14½ miles from Aigle takes just over an hour.

The metre gauge AOMC opened from Aigle to Monthey-Ville on 2nd April, 1907 and from Monthey-Ville to the CFF station on 1st April, 1909, but has long been replaced by buses. It was operated electrically with a 850v DC supply from the outset. The rack and pinion section uses the Strub system.

The Aigle-Sepey-Diablerets (ASD) is the only 'non-rack' member of the Transport Publics du Chablis (TPC) an association formed on 1st July, 1977 with local communities which placed the Aigle-Leysin (AL), ASD, AOMC and the Bex-Villars-Bretaye (BVB) under one Direction with the aim of better use of resources and integration of their rail and road services.

Pinion-fitted BDeh 4/4 1 with its driving trailer stands at Aigle on 30th June, 1992. Trains of the Aigle-Leysin line can be seen alongside the Federal Railways' station at which a train has just arrived. *Alan Pike*

Old and new stand at the Monthey terminus on 28th July, 1990. Bdeh 4/4 1 was built in 1987 while Bdeh 4/4 11 dates from 1954. Trains reverse here and retrace their route for some way before joining the rack to climb to Champéry. *Alan Pike*

BDeh 4/4 14 waits at Champéry to return to Monthey on 12th August, 1993. The line had not long been extended to this rather bleak platform to enable skiers to join the large cable cars to take them to the ski slopes in winter. *Alan Pike*

Chemin de fer Aigle-Leysin (AL)

The second rack-and-adhesion railway to start from the square at Aigle is the one to Leysin, a resort at 4,150 feet which overlooks the Rhône valley, and in addition to all its facilities for summer and winter holidays, hosts an international academy of music. It was noted as a suitable place for the treatment of TB. Some British servicemen were sent there immediately after World War II. Leysin was also where British service personnel who escaped to Switzerland were interned in most benign conditions.

This metre gauge railway opened from the CFF station to the depot on 5th May, 1900, and from there to Leysin-Feydey on 6th November, 1900. The extension to Grand-Hotel came much later on 12th September, 1916. The Abt system was chosen for the rack and pinion section and power supply was 650v DC from the opening until 1946 when it became 1,300v DC.

The brown and cream-coloured railcars of the railway pass through the streets of the town and across the Grande Eau, then, after reversing at the depot, take to the rack-and-pinion on a gradient of 1 in 4½ to ascend through the woods and vineyards along the western side of the Vallée des Ormonts. After a stop at Leysin-Feydey, the train then goes through a tunnel which leads to the terminus at the Leysin-Grand-Hotel. Its glory has faded, and for a long time this station has seen few passengers, for the hotel is no longer in use as such. However, a proposal to extend the line to a nearby cable car terminal much used by skiers may well succeed. The train has taken 35 minutes to make the journey from Aigle, having climbed 3,252 feet in doing so.

The Aigle-Leysin depot on 12th August, 1993. After running through the streets of the town, trains reverse here before picking up the rack for the climb to Leysin. *Alan Pike*

Bdeh 2/4 201 waits for passengers from a connecting Swiss Federal Railways train at Aigle on 30th June, 1992. *Alan Pike*

Be4/4 305, a modern unit of the Aigle-Leysin railway, seen here at Aigle depot which is also where the climb on the rack section begins, having left the street-running in Aigle. *Les Heath*

Chemin de fer Bex-Villars-Bretaye (BVB)

The town of Bex is situated on the Swiss Federal Railways' Simplon line and is no more than a few minutes from St Maurice, where the abbey, founded in the year 370, commemorates the saint to whom it is dedicated. This line is the lower section of the Bex-Villars-Bretaye Bahn. The line begins outside the station of the Swiss Federal Railways at Bex and passes along the main street to Bevieux. Here the climb to Gryon begins on a gradient of 1 in 5, with rack-and-pinion working all the way. Just before Gryon station the rack finishes. 'In-road' and roadside running commences and after passing through La Barboleuse, crosses the Gryonne gorge on a viaduct 165 feet high which also carries a roadway, and soon afterwards brings the traveller to Villars-sur-Ollon.

The red or red and white motor coaches have taken 45 minutes to make the journey from Bex, and in so doing have climbed 2,710 feet to one of the most popular mountain ski resorts in French Switzerland. The view from the esplanade south-westward to the Dents du Midi and the Mont Blanc group is wonderful.

The upper section of the Bex-Villars-Bretaye Railway, ascends from Villars-sur-Ollon to the Col-de-Bretaye in 20 minutes. It is normally run as a seperate section although there is a direct connection at Villars with the main system.

The Col-de-Bretaye line, two and a half miles long, has a ruling gradient of 1 in 6, and its trains climb to a height of 5,932 feet. This is a famous skiing area, with many hoists, and runs which attract visitors throughout the winter and in summer provides many easy walks. A new golf course between Col de Sud and Bouqueting attracts international attention.

The BVB is also a member of the TPC (*see page 53*). This metre gauge line opened from Bex to Bevieux on 10th September, 1898 and this section is still run as a tramway, the small blue tram-type cars making many more stops than the through cars to Villars. Bevieux to Gryon opened on 4th June, 1900, Gryon to Villars on 16th June, 1901 and Villars to Bretaye on 18th December, 1913.

It was electrically operated from the outset the supply being 700v DC. The Abt rack system is used.

A solitary BDeh 2/4 23 built in 1941 is in the 'old' livery as it stands outside the Federal Railways' station at Bex on 20th April, 1998. *Alan Pike*

Bdeh 2/4 24 built in 1941 sports the 'old' red livery as it waits to return from Villars to Bex on 23rd June, 1995. *Alan Pike*

End of track at Villars on 23rd June, 1995. The line originally continued ahead in the public road to the next village of Chesières. The track in the centre foreground is one of the two at Villars which links the Bex line with the Bretaye line. The 1977 stock and the only unit bought in 1988 show the considerable change in style over a short period. *Alan Pike*

The snow is beginning to melt at Bretaye on 20th April, 1998 as BDeh 4/4 83 is about to take the last train of the day back to Villars. *Alan Pike*

The Villars-Bretaye section. The panoramic driving trailer was introduced in the summer of 1998, the panoramic coach came into service winter of 1998/1999. The train is seen here departing from Villars station with skiers going to Bretaye on 1st March, 1999. *Les Heath*

The new liveries of the Bex-Bevieux adhesion-only car, Be2/3 16 of 1948, in the blue and white livery, contrasts with the bold red and yellow livery of pinion-fitted BDeh 2/4 25 dating from 1944. On 29th October, 1994, the former is waiting outside Bex Federal Railways' station for passengers for the town of Bex whilst the latter will continue over rack and adhesion sections to Villars. Shunter He 2/2 2 of 1900 can be seen in the background.   *Alan Pike*

La Barboleuse on the BVB in March 1999. All pinion-fitted units can operate on both lines from Bex to Bretaye. The power car is one of three, the first of which was introduced in 1977.   *Les Heath*

Chemin de fer Martigny-Châtelard (MC)

The metre-gauge Martigny-Châtelard trains start from a bay platform at the western end of the Simplon main line station at Martigny, a town situated at the point where the Rhône makes a right-angle turn to the north and heads for Montreux. The line runs in sight of the Swiss Federal Simplon metals as far as Vernayaz, then turns away from the Rhône valley on a climb with a gradient of 1 in 5, which involves the use of the Strub rack-and-pinion system until the village of Salvan is reached.

The train is now in the Trient valley and calls at Les Marécottes and Le Trétien before negotiating a truly spectacular section of the line, on the edge of a precipice with the valley floor 1,400 feet below. Once past Finhaut, the line descends to Le Châtelard-Frontière before crossing into France and arriving in Vallorcine. At one time, the driving trailer of one of the trains was transferred to a metre-gauge train of the French Railways (SNCF) for the journey to Argentière, Chamonix-Mont Blanc and St Gervais-Fayet but most through passengers had to change, bringing useful custom to the small café on the platform. Through working has been restored with the advent of five 2-car sets built in Switzerland, three owned by the MC and two by the SNCF. They are 'panorama' style and like the repainted older sets, stand out boldly in red and white livery. They were introduced into regular service in 1997, enabling four daily return journeys from Martigny to St Gervais-les-Bains Fayet, each single journey taking about two hours, thanks to a top speed of 70 kph. Timings vary by a few minutes. There is also one return journey to Chamonix. All these services are called 'Mont Blanc Express'.

Techinically the line is of particular interest in that the section from Martigny to Vernayaz has overhead line equipment. At Vernayaz a change is made to third rail, similar to its SNCF partner. At one time it went all the way to Vallorcine but is gradually being replaced in Switzerland by overhead except in the tunnel between Vernayaz and Salvin.

The line opened from Martigny to Le Châtelard Frontière on 20th August, 1906 but ran through the town of Martigny. Connection between Le Châtelard and the Paris-Lyon-Mediterranée (later SNCF) took place at Vallorcine on 2nd July, 1908, but it was not until 1st March, 1931 that the direct line from Martigny CFF to La Bâtiaz was opened. The line continues to be electrically operated at 800v DC.

The ascent of the Brévent from Chamonix is made by a cableway completed in 1930. This is in two sections, and the upper one is 4,440 feet long without an intermediate pylon. At one point the traveller finds himself 1,000 feet up in the air, an experience not recommended to those unaccustomed to aerial cableways.

Logo of the Chemin de fer Martigny-Châtelard, August 1996.   *Alan Pike*

A Martigny-Châtelard train in Martigny station in July 1975.   *Author*

Martigny-Châtelard trains passing at Le Trétien in July 1975.   *Author*

The station at Argentière, France, on the Vallorcine to Chamonix line in July 1975.   *Author*

A train from Vallorcine on arrival at Chamonix, France, July 1975.   *Author*

Beautifully restored ABDeh 4/4 32 built in 1921 stands at Vernayaz on 15th August, 1996. The shoe gear for use over the third rail sections can be clearly seen on both bogies.   *Alan Pike*

Some idea of the nature of the terrain can be gathered from this view of BDeh 4/4 5 leaving for Le Châtelard-Frontière on 21st April, 1998. The pantograph has been lowered because current is now being taken from the third rail.   *Alan Pike*

A general view of Vernayaz works and depot on 17th August, 1996 shows, from left to right, one of the two 4-wheel electric shunters which entered service in 1962, ABDeh 4/4 320f 1921 and BDeh 4/4 8 delivered in 1964. *Alan Pike*

Interior of one of the articulated 'panorama' sets which work through trains from Martigny to St Gervais-Fayet in France under the 'Mont Blanc Express' title. They are permitted to operate at 70 kmh where appropriate. The picture was taken on 29th April, 1997. *Alan Pike*

Abt system 0-4-2T No. 2 *Monte Rosa* of the Visp-Zermatt railway *c.* 1930. *J.W.B. Tunstall*

Brig-Visp-Zermatt trains passing at Kalpetran, July 1973. *Author*

Brig-Visp-Zermatt Bahn (BVZ)

The metre-gauge Visp-Zermatt line was completed in 1891, and was expanded from Visp to Brig, parallel to the Swiss Federal Railway tracks, on 5th June, 1930 - a total distance of 27 miles, covered by the express trains in 87 minutes and two of the Glacier Expresses in 80 minutes. The line is controlled by colour-light signals operated from Brig, and there are several lengths requiring rack-and-pinion using the Abt system between Visp and Zermatt, with a ruling gradient of 1 in 8. The railway was operated by steam locomotives until 1st October, 1929 when it was electrified at 11kv 16.7Hz; the same as the Furka-Oberalp and the Rhätischebahn.

The Brig-Visp-Zermatt and the Furka-Oberalp Bahnen share a station in Brig. It is situated in the square outside the main Swiss Federal building, and the bright red trains of the concerns contribute to a lively and fascinating scene.

The railway leaves the valley of the Rhône at Visp, turning south towards the highest part of the Nikolaital. Four miles along the line, the steepest section is reached at Stalden-Saas, and soon the track is bordered on each side by mountains as it wends its way up the valley of the Matter-Visp. At Herbriggen in 1991 a huge section of the mountainside collapsed in two stages. The first fortunately gave a warning to those in the houses threatened by the slide and there were no casualities. Road and rail communications were severed and the BVZ had to build a diversion of some 3 km involving two new sections of rack. The consequences of this massive collapse are likely to be visible for many years. At Randa the Breithorn comes into view at the head of the valley, and then, no more than half a mile from journey's end, the Matterhorn.

At Täsch an enormous car and coach park has been established because, apart from a few special permit holders, no internal-combustion-engined road vehicles are allowed in Zermatt. This is good business for the BVZ which runs a frequent shuttle service over the intervening 6 km.

The incomparable Matterhorn towers above Zermatt, and in the graveyard of the parish church are the memorial stones for four of the seven climbers who lost their lives on 14th July, 1865. They were members of the first expedition, led by Edward Whymper, to reach the summit of the mountain, and were on the descent when their life-line snapped.

There is a physical connection at Zermatt between the BVZ and the Gornergratbahn used for the transfer of freight.

A Brig-Visp-Zermatt train leaving Brig in June 1973.   *Author*

67

A southbound train in the Matter-Visp gorge in July 1973.   *Author*

The metre-gauge station at Brig, July 1973.   *Author*

Furka-Oberalp Bahn (FO)

The first section of this metre-gauge railway was opened in 1915, between Brig and Gletsch, but not until 1926 was it finally completed via Andermatt to Disentis, where it makes an end-on junction with the Rhätischebahn. Ten steam locomotives were built in 1913 to operate the line. They were 2-6-0T engines and were built at Winterthur by Schweizerische Lokomotiv - und Maschinen Fabrik. One of them, No. 4, survives and is kept at Münster. Another is on the Blonay-Chamby line whilst the Dampfbahn-Furka-Bergstrecke (DFB) has four, Nos. 1, 2, 8 and 9, recovered from Vietnam, to which country they had been sold in 1947. Two have been restored (1998) and are in service between Realp and Furka on the old line over the Furka. It is the aim of the preservation society to reinstate the whole line between Realp and Oberwald. Work has concentrated at the Realp end but progress is now being made in the Gletsch area.

The Furka-Oberalp Bahn was electrified between 1940 and 1942 at 11kv 16.7Hz. From its junction at Brig with the line from Zermatt, the route proceeds via Fiesch, Niederwald and Münster to Oberwald. The famous hotelier César Ritz was born at Niederwald in 1850, and there, too, he was buried.

A new tunnel, completed in 1992, commences at Oberwald. Almost 10 miles in length, and the longest wholly in Switzerland, that is until the Vereina tunnel on the Rhätischebahn, just under 12 miles long, opens in November 1999. The tunnel avoids the long climb via Gletsch to the summit at Furka, and the equally steep descent to Realp at the eastern end of the bore. The Furka-Oberalp can now stay open throughout the year, an impossibility in days gone by, but passengers on the railway can no longer see the Rhône glacier near Gletsch. This beautiful ice-fall has been gradually shrinking but is still a grand and impressive sight.

Some five miles beyond Realp the railway approaches Andermatt, and here it is joined by the Schöllenen Bahn, which climbs from Göschenen, on the Gotthard line more than 1,000 feet below. It was opened in 1917, but was not taken over by the Furka-Oberalp until 1960. Equipped with the Abt double rack system, its ruling gradient is 1 in 5½, and the sight of one of its trains approaching Göschenen at the end of its descent through the Schöllenen gorge is well worth a wait.

From Andermatt, the Furka-Oberalp begins its climb to the final summit at Oberalppasshöhe, 6,670 feet above sea level. Thence comes the descent via Tschamut-Selva and Sedrun to Disentis, named Mustér in the Romansch language. The Benedictine Abbey at Disentis was founded by Saint Sigisbert c. 720, and its Baroque church of Saint Martin was completed in 1712.

Nowadays, the principal 'Glacier Express' takes approximately 7¾ hours for the journey from Zermatt to St Moritz, compared with 8¼ hours twenty years ago, and in the summer months additional 'Glacier Expresses' are called for. From Disentis to St Moritz, the trains run on the lines of the Rhätischebahn, which also provides the locomotives.

A westbound train on the Furka-Oberalp Railway in July 1973.   *Author*

A Furka-Oberalp train ready to leave Brig for Andermatt in July 1973. *Author*

On 2nd May 1997, a 'Glacier Express' winds down the rack into Andermatt on its way to Brig and Zermatt hauled by HGe 4/4 104 *Furka* built in 1986. *Alan Pike*

Unusually, a pinion-fitted locomotive HGe 4/4″ 101 arrives from Oberwald at Realp on the car carrier train on 5th November, 1995 rather than one of the two locomotives specifically built for the service through the Furka Basis tunnel which are not equipped as the rack this is not required in the tunnel.   *Alan Pike*

A 'panoramic' coach brings up the rear of a Brig to Disentis train which is about to leave Realp on 12th July, 1998.   *Alan Pike*

Deh4/4 52 with a train travelling down the rack section from Andermatt to Göschenen. The line contains several tunnel sections and long covered galleries to protect the train from snow and falling rocks.   *Les Heath*

A Deh 4/4, one of five built in 1972, calls at Realp on a train for Göschenen on 5th November, 1995.   *Alan Pike*

The Dampfbahn Furka Bergstrecke is a preservation line devoted to the re-opening of the old FO line over the Furka Pass and through the now high level tunnel. Dampfbahn Furka Bergstrecke 2-6-0 rack tank No. 2 on the depot of the preservation railway at Realp before taking a train up to the entrance of the old Furka tunnel on 12th July, 1998. *Alan Pike*

Dampfbahn Furka Bergstrecke 2-6-0 rack tank No. 2 built by SLM in 1914 for the FO has just arrived at Furka station at the eastern end of the old Furka tunnel on 12th July, 1998 after climbing from Realp. *Alan Pike*

St Gallen-Gais-Appenzell (SGA)

This metre-gauge railway begins from a station alongside that of the Swiss Federal Railways in the city of St Gallen, in north-east Switzerland. Not far from the terminus, the assistance of Riggenbach/Klose system rack-and-pinion is required on a gradient of 1 in 6¼, the first of several sections on which rack-and-pinion working is necessary on the journey. The beautifully-situated village of Teufen is home to the headquarters of the railway, and here the Santis comes into view. From the summit, 8,215 feet in height, the mountain commands a magnificent panorama of the Vorarlberg mountains, the Grisons Alps, Glarus, the Bernese Alps and the Lakes of Zurich and Constance.

At Gais, 12½ miles from St Gallen, the railway reaches its maximum altitude of 3,077 feet. Gais is not only the location of the Works of the SGA but is a junction where an SGA branch, an independent railway until 1948, diverges to the left, to climb briefly to Stoss and then descend steeply, with Strub rack-and-pinion operation, to the valley of the Rhine and the town of Altstätten. This is a journey of some seven miles, accomplished in 20 minutes, and on the way there is a wonderful view of the Rhine valley. Until 1975, the railway ran through the narrow streets of the ancient town to the SBB station where there were exchange sidings. Increased road traffic led to the truncation of the line on the edge of the town.

The railway that continues from Gais to Appenzell is mostly on a downward gradient, with rack-and-pinion operation again employed. Arrival at Appenzell is over a handsome viaduct, after a journey from St Gallen that has occupied an average of 45 minutes, with 12 potential intermediate stops on the way.

The line from St Gallen to Gais opened on 1st October, 1889 and from Gais to Appenzell on 1st July, 1904. The Gais-Altstätten Stadt dates from 18th November, 1911, and the extension from Stadt to the SBB station operated from 26th June, 1912 to 31st May, 1975. The absorbed Altstätten-Gais line was electrified at 1,500v DC from the outset, but it was not until 23rd January, 1931 that electric operation began between St Gallen and Appenzell. After many years of common management, the SGA merged in 1988 with the Appenzeller Bahn (AB) to form the Appenzeller Bahnen.

The SGA ran through the narrow streets of Altstätten to the Federal Railways' station until increasing road traffic forced its truncation on the outskirts of town. The connection is maintained by bus. *Alan Pike*

Trains cross at Gais on 1st March, 1989. That to the right is for St Gallen while that at the left goes to Appenzell. Gais is the location for the SGA depot and works. The SGA merged in 1988 with the all adhesion Appenzeller Bahn to form the Appenzeller Bahnen.   *Alan Pike*

Appenzeller Bahnen BDeh 4/4 15, ex-SGA, in advertising livery, stands at the terminus the AB shares with the Trogener Bahn close by the Federal Railways' station at St Gallen in the late evening of 14th July, 1998.   *Alan Pike*

Rorschach-Heiden-Bahn (RHB)

Rorschach stands on the shore of the Bodensee (Lake Constance), and is the largest port on the Swiss side of the lake. In 1875, a standard-gauge rack and adhesion railway was opened from Rorschach to Heiden, a village in the hills a little over 3½ miles distant, which *Bradshaw* in years gone by called 'an air-cure and whey-cure resort'. Its location away from the humidity of the Bodensee area, encouraged development as a 'dormitory' village for St Gallen. The red Rorschach-Heiden Bahn coaches make the ascent from Rorschach Hafen (Harbour) station to Heiden in 23 minutes, using the Swiss Federal (SBB) tracks from the Harbour to Rorschach. Thus, for two minutes of their journey, the Rorschach-Heiden coaches share lines used by international expresses.

Passenger ships belonging to the SBB and DBAG cross the lake from Rorschach to Lindau, which lies in Germany, close to the border with Austria. The voyage takes an hour and a quarter. Amongst the attractions of this island town is the Zeppelin museum. It was on the 2nd July, 1900, that Count Ferdinand von Zeppelin's first dirigible started its maiden flight from Friedrichshafen on Lake Constance.

DZeh2/4 22 built by SLM in 1930 is seen at Heiden on 17th April, 1976. *Alan Pike*

ABDeh2/4 is seen at Rorschach station in July 1998.   *Alan Pike*

ABDeh2/4 24 about to leave Heiden for Rorschach in July 1998.   *Alan Pike*

ABDeh2/4 24 and to the left DZeh2/4 22 built in 1930 are seen at Heiden on 8th November, 1998. *Alan Pike*

This new unit came into service in February 1999. It is seen here at Rorschach Hafen station on 2nd March, 1999. *Les Heath*

Acknowledgements

I am most grateful to Alan Pike for his kindness in providing much information regarding developments in recent years on the Swiss rack railways. I would also like to thank him, together with Les Heath and Roger Kidner, for their willing and valuable help with photographs from their collections.

Bibliography

Switzerland's Amazing Railways, Allen, Cecil J. , Thomas Nelson, 1953.

Swiss Travel Wonderland, Allen, Cecil J., Ian Allan, 1972.

Railway Holiday in Switzerland, Behrend, George, David and Charles / Macdonald, 1965.

Steam over Switzerland, Behrend, George, Jersey Artists, 1973.

Metre Gauge Railways in South and East Switzerland, Marshall, John, David and Charles, 1974.

Railways in the Bernese Oberland, Bairstow, Martin, 1987.

Baedeker's Switzerland, Karl Baedeker, 1967

Bernese Oberland and Lucerne, Muirhead, L. Russell, Ernest Benn, 1963, Blue Guide.

Michelin's Switzerland, Michelin Tourist Services, 1972.

Swiss Official Timetables, Various Editions: (Editor, Swiss Federal Railways).

Die Gotthard Bahn, Marti, Franz and Trüb, Walter, Orell Füssli Verlag, Zürich, 1971

Die Rhätische Bahn, Marti, Franz and Trüb, Walter, Orell Füssli Verlag, Zürich, 1972.

Bern Lötschberg Simplon 60th Anniversary Booklet, BLS, Bern, 1973.

Paddle Steamers of the Alps, Brown, Leslie and McKendrick, Joe, Ferry Publications.

Grosses Eisenbahn Atlas, Schweiz, Kummerley & Frey, Bern.

Editions 'Revue des Amis du Rail' Aigle.

Swiss Railways European Handbook, Platform 5 Publishing Ltd, Sheffield, 1997.

Lokomotiven und Triebwagen der Schweizer Bahnen, P. Willen, Orell Füssli Verlag, Zürich.

Schienenwetz Schweiz, AS Verlag, Zürich 1998.